SURVIVING YOUR DWI

in Cooke County

Deandra M. Grant, JD, GC, MS
ACS-CHAL Forensic Lawyer-Scientist
Managing Partner

Douglas E. Huff, JD
ACS-CHAL Forensic Lawyer-Scientist
Partner

Offices Conveniently Located in
Dallas | Denton | Austin | Allen | Fort Worth | Waco

ISBNS:
PAPERBACK: 978-1-964281-16-2
EBOOK: 978-1-964281-17-9

DISCLAIMER

The information in this book does NOT constitute legal advice. You can only obtain sound legal advice from a lawyer who has been given the specific facts of your case. Every case is different.

Please note that our lawyers are happy to consult with you if you do decide to obtain legal advice. However, please understand that simply reading this book does not form an attorney-client relationship with our firm or with any of the authors.

Table of Contents

Meet the Authors

Meet Deandra M. Grant, JD, GC, MS:

Deandra M. Grant

Deandra Grant was born in Denton, but grew up in Plano, and is a proud graduate of Plano Senior High School. A native Texan, her family has lived for generations in and around Gainesville, Texas.

Deandra's hard-nosed work ethic began at an early age with a variety of teenage jobs: social director at a teen nightclub, clerk at a dress shop, and owner/ manager of a New Orleans-style sno-cone stand (Mr Sno Ball!), to name a few.

After high school she attended Trinity University in San Antonio, then came back home to Dallas for law school at SMU. Deandra has been married to Eric Clendenin for over 20 years and they have two children, Keegan and Rowan.

When not practicing law, she is very involved with dog rescue and serves as vice president of Living the Doxie Dream Rescue & Sanctuary, in Royse City. At home she and Eric have five rescue dachshunds, and you can follow their adventures on their Instagram page, @5WienerPack.

Deandra is a huge Van Halen fan (DLR – not Hagar), studies medieval European history as a hobby, and loves to travel.

Lawyer Stuff:

Deandra was included in the list of Super Lawyers® for 2011, 2012, and 2015 through 2023. Super Lawyers is an attorney rating service that is nationally recognized throughout the legal community. After performing exhaustive and rigorous research by an independent research team, they announce their list of highly capable, trustworthy, and competent attorneys in *Super Lawyers* magazine and online. The list represents no more than 5% of the attorneys in Texas.

Deandra is AV Preeminent Rated by Martindale-Hubbell, which is the highest rating an attorney can achieve. She was given the AV rating for her outstanding professional achievements in the field of DWI law and her contributions to the legal community. She's also been rated 10.0 by both AVVO and Justia.

Deandra began work on *The Texas DWI Manual* in 2011 for James Publishing. She calls it her "labor of love." The first edition was released in 2013. It is updated annually and is considered a "must have" for attorneys defending DWI cases in Texas.

Experience

Deandra graduated in 1990 from Trinity University in San Antonio with a B.S. in Business Administration. She earned her law degree from the SMU School of Law and was licensed by the State Bar of Texas in 1993. Having spent her last year of law school as an intern with the Dallas County District Attorney's Office, she began work there as an assistant district attorney in January 1994.

Deandra's tenure as a prosecutor focused on DWI prosecution. In 1995, she founded her own firm and began defending citizens accused of DWI and other crimes. She has practiced criminal defense for over 30 years and represents Texans charged with criminal offenses, including DWI, violent felonies, and sex crimes. As a former prosecutor, she knows firsthand how to counter the prosecutor's evidence and strategy.

Operator and Testing Experience

Deandra has spent hundreds of hours in training courses and programs related to DWI defense. She has participated in numerous "dosing" experiments in which people are given specific amounts of alcohol over certain time periods and then tested to see the effect of the alcohol on their mental and physical capabilities. She attended and successfully completed the operator certification course for the Intoxilyzer 5000 in Florida in 2004. This was the breath-test machine used in Texas prior to the purchase of the Intoxilyzer 9000. She learned how to operate the machine and the science behind it. She has also participated in experiments related to the inaccuracy of the machine.

Deandra has completed both the student course (2008) and the instructor course (2009) on the administration of standardized field sobriety testing (SFST), the same National Highway Traffic Safety Administration training course that teaches police officers nationwide how to identify drunk drivers during traffic stops. She now serves as an instructor of the SFST practitioner course to share the knowledge with other attorneys. In 2008, she completed coursework in Atlanta, Georgia, on DWI forensic blood and urine testing.

In 2011, she began training at Axion Labs in Chicago. The courses include Forensic Chromatography, Forensic Drug Analysis, and Forensic Driving Under the Influence of Drugs. She completed the coursework, passed the final exam in

2015, and was awarded the American Chemical Society Forensic Lawyer-Scientist designation. In 2018, Deandra joined Axion Labs as an assistant chromatography instructor. She spends five weeks each year in Chicago at the lab.

In 2014, Deandra "went back to school." She completed a Graduate Certificate in Forensic Toxicology from the University of Florida's College of Veterinary Medicine, and a master's degree in Pharmaceutical Science – Concentration in Forensic Science from the University of Florida's College of Pharmacy, in 2016.

Deandra is a national speaker and teacher on topics including trial skills, jury selection, cross examination, field sobriety tests, drugged driving, and forensic breath and blood alcohol testing. Since 2019, she's been honored to serve on the faculty of the Robert F. Borkenstein Course on the Effects of Drugs on Human Performance and Behavior.

Meet Douglas E. Huff, JD:

Douglas E. Huff

Attorney Douglas Huff was born in Warren, Ohio, and was raised in Western Pennsylvania, outside of Pittsburgh, where he attended Mount Pleasant Area High School. After high school, Attorney Huff enlisted in the United States Army and served for four years, receiving both the Army Achievement Medal and the Army Commendation Medal. He received an honorable discharge after completing his full term of service and relocated to Austin, Texas.

After attending law school, Doug worked at Barbri, an organization specializing in assisting law students in studying and passing the state bar examination. In addition to being licensed to practice law in the state of Texas, he sat and passed the Oklahoma Bar during this time. Afterward, he opened his own law practice, The Law Office of Douglas E. Huff, in Dallas, Texas, where he represented clients charged with various misdemeanor and felony criminal offenses.

In 2013, Doug accepted a position with the Dallas County Public Defender's Office, where he worked diligently as the lead attorney in many DWI trials and other misdemeanor cases. Additionally, he has assisted numerous clients through plea negotiations, led many evidentiary hearings, and prepared and taken part in felony trials.

Attorney Huff joined Deandra Grant Law in 2016. He became a partner in 2021. Doug is based in the Dallas office, but practices throughout Texas.

On a personal note, Doug has one daughter (attorney Sorsha Huff) and a rescue dog named Athena. He's a military vet who loves to travel. One of his favorite trips was walking the Camino de Santiago, in Spain. Doug is also a competitive poker player whom you can often find playing in tournaments around the country.

Introduction

So, you've been arrested for DWI in Cooke County and you're wondering, "What next?"

This book walks you through the steps you need to take to deal with both the driver's license issues and criminal charges you face.

County Information

Cooke County Courthouse
101 S. Dixon St
Gainesville, TX 76240

Bond Supervision	(940) 668-5540

MISDEMEANOR COURT:

County Court at Law	(940) 668-5470	2nd floor

FELONY COURT:

235th District Court	(940) 668-5401	2nd floor

What to Expect

Step #1: Department of Public Safety

- Make sure the address on your driver's license is correct. If it's not, you need to go to the DPS website and update your address.

- Check your mail regularly for letters from the Department of Public Safety (DPS).

The DPS will mail any letters to you at the address they have on file. If you have moved, or don't frequently check your mail, you could miss time-sensitive letters regarding your right to challenge the suspension of your driver's license, which can aggravate your situation.

We often see new clients who, prior to coming to us, have already missed their opportunity to challenge a driver's license suspension following a DWI arrest, either because the DPS did not have their correct address when mailing a notice of the hearing or the client did not regularly check incoming mail. Too often, these clients are unaware that they are driving with a suspended license until they are caught and charged.

Step #2: Cooke County Bond Conditions

- Comply with any and all bond conditions ordered by the judge who sets your bond.

If there was an accident, a breath or blood alcohol content result of 0.15 or greater, or if you have had prior DWIs, the judge will likely order that a deep lung device (DLD) be installed on any car that you drive. You MUST contact the Bond Supervision Department within the timeframe noted on your court order/bond conditions and set up an appointment. You are required to pay to have the unit installed and provide proof to your bond supervision officer. You will also be required to report in, and pay a monthly supervision fee, while your case is pending.

We sometimes have clients who were involved in accidents and no longer have a car to drive. In that case, your bond supervision officer will likely order that an alcohol monitoring device be installed in your home instead of your car. You will be required to blow into this device at specific times in order to demonstrate that you are not drinking alcohol while on bond.

Failure to comply with bond conditions can lead to your bond being held insufficient and a warrant issued for your arrest.

If you took a breath test and the result was 0.15 or greater, OR if you had blood drawn and the result was 0.15 or greater, but an interlock device was NOT added as a condition of bond when you bonded out of jail, do not be surprised if, at your first court appearance, the judge handling your criminal case orders you to install one.

Step #3: Administrative License Revocation

- Request an ALR hearing within 15 days

If you refused to provide a specimen of your breath or blood after your DWI arrest, you have 15 days from the date you received notice of suspension to request a hearing. Notice of suspension is typically handed to you by the police officer or included in your paperwork when you bond out of jail.

If you consented to a blood test, the clock doesn't start ticking until the Department of Public Safety (DPS) sends you a notice of suspension. However, we see a lot of mistakes made by officers, such as labeling your charge a "failure," meaning you refused to consent to a test when in fact your blood was taken with your consent. That mistake can cost you.

You can request the hearing yourself, or your attorney can request it for you. If you fail to request the hearing within the 15-day timeframe, however, your right to a hearing is forfeit and your license will be suspended on the 40th day after notice of suspension was served.

Step #4: Cooke County Court Appearances

- Establish when and where you are required to appear in court

Cooke County has seven county (misdemeanor case) and seven district (felony case) courts, all located in the Cooke County Courthouse. See the preceding chapter for a directory indicating which courts are on which floors.

Cooke County judges typically require you to appear at all court settings, even if charged in misdemeanor court.

It is not uncommon in Cooke for there to be a large number of cases on each docket, so plan to be in court for most of the morning. Cases in Cooke County tend to move faster than those in surrounding counties.

Step #5: Disposition Meeting

- Meet with your attorney to decide how to proceed

At Deandra Grant Law, we first write a case evaluation that summarizes all of the evidence in the case for you and gives you our overall opinion of your case. Once you have had the opportunity to review our case evaluation and watch any videos from your arrest, we schedule a disposition meeting where we sit down with you to discuss achieving the best outcome for you. At that meeting, we decide together whether that best outcome is to accept a plea bargain or take your case to trial.

Step #6: Plea Docket or Trial Docket

- Schedule a plea date or a trial date, depending on how you decide to proceed with your case, and appear on the scheduled date and time. Cooke County does not distinguish between a plea docket and a trial docket; instead, courts follow a set schedule of all court appearances from first appearance to trial, once a case is filed. However, cases can be pled prior to trial if a plea agreement is reached.

After your disposition meeting, it is time to determine whether the case will be settled by plea, or whether it will proceed to the trial date. In Cooke, you must appear on all scheduled dates.

Plea Date

If you choose to enter into a plea bargain with the State, you must appear in court on your plea court date.

Take a seat inside the courtroom and wait for your attorney to arrive. Once the plea paperwork is completed, you enter your plea in front of the judge. It might be the presiding judge or a visiting judge who takes your plea.

If you are placed on probation, you will meet with a probation officer after you enter your plea and the clerks complete your paperwork. The clerks are normally in the courtroom during the plea. The probation department is in the same building, and a representative from probation will begin your intake into probation immediately after your plea is entered. The probation representative may give you additional instructions on what to do and where to go after the probation intake.

The whole process takes several hours, so plan to be at the courthouse until noon or later.

Trial Announcement

Cases set for trial in Cooke County will proceed to a trial announcement date, which is scheduled one to two weeks before the trial date. At trial announcement, both the State (prosecution) and the Defense will announce "Ready" or "Not Ready" for trial. Pre-trial issues/rulings are typically addressed at an earlier setting, but the judge may handle any remaining that need to be made before the trial begins.

At trial announcement, the judge will let the attorneys know which cases are likely to go to trial the following week and which ones will be rescheduled.

Trial Date

On your trial date you must appear at the time ordered by the judge and wait for your attorney to meet you in court.

If your case is reached, your trial will normally begin that day and may last one to three days, depending on many factors.

DWI FAQs

Q: **When I was arrested for DWI in Cooke County, I received a piece of paper that said my driver's license is suspended. Is my license now suspended?**

A: No. *You have 15 days from the date you are served your Notice of Suspension to request an administrative license revocation (ALR) hearing regarding your driver's license.* If you do not request a hearing, your license will be suspended on the 40th day after Notice of Suspension is served. It is important to seek the advice of an attorney regarding your driver's license issues before this 15-day window expires.

If you consented to a blood draw, a Notice of Suspension will be mailed to you if the DPS (Department of Public Safety) receives notice that your blood alcohol analysis resulted in an alcohol concentration of 0.08 or greater. *Once you receive this Notice of Suspension letter from DPS, you only have 20 days from the date of the letter to request an ALR hearing.* If you do not request a hearing, your license will be suspended on the 45th day from the date on the Notice of Suspension letter.

Q: **For my DWI arrest, I was ordered to install a deep lung device (DLD) on my car as a condition of bond. What do I have to do, and is that my only option?**

A: In certain circumstances, a DLD may be required while your case is pending. There may be alternatives that would work for you. We can tell you more when we sit down with you to examine the specific circumstances of your case.

Q: When do I have to go to court on my DWI for the first time, if it's a misdemeanor case?

A: In Cooke County, misdemeanor cases are normally filed within one to two months after your arrest. In some circumstances, it may take longer for your case to be filed. You will need to retain an attorney immediately after your arrest to begin work on your driver's license issues.

Q: How long will it take to resolve my DWI case in Cooke County?

A: Cooke County cases are typically filed one to two months after the arrest, and follow Scheduling Order, which sets out all of the court dates over the next five to six months, including a trial date. Cases where a plea bargain is worked out can be resolved prior to the jury trial date. However, there are many other factors that can determine how long a criminal case will last. Cases that are on the trial docket obviously take longer to resolve than cases where a plea bargain is worked out. The majority of our DWI cases are resolved within four to seven months in Cooke County.

Q: Will I go to prison or jail for my DWI?

A: The punishment varies, depending upon the circumstances of your particular case, and whether this is your first, second, or subsequent offense. When you work with a defense lawyer and fight your charges, you may have the opportunity to avoid a conviction and remain free.

Q: **How can an attorney help me with my DWI in Cooke County?**

A: An attorney works knowledgeably and skillfully to protect your rights and interests by challenging the prosecution's case and the evidence against you. This may include challenges to field sobriety test results, breath test results, or blood test results. An attorney's representation also includes being present, either at your side or on your behalf, at any and all court appearances, including trial.

An attorney will also work on your driver's license issues and help you deal with any possible license suspension.

Q: **Can a lawyer represent me at my Cooke County ALR hearing?**

A: Yes. We can contact the Department of Public Safety to schedule your administrative license revocation (ALR) hearing and represent you at the hearing in order to help you reach a better outcome. Your driving privileges are extremely important, and skilled representation at your hearing may mean the difference between you keeping those privileges or losing them.

Q: What are some penalties associated with a Cooke County DWI conviction?

A: Specific penalties vary, but, in general, a defendant may face imprisonment, probation, community service, driver's license suspension, fines, and more.

Q: If I have a DWI conviction on my record, can this affect my ability to find employment?

A: It is possible that having a DWI conviction on your criminal record may make it more difficult for you to find employment. When a potential employer conducts a pre-employment background search, your DWI conviction will show up. This may or may not affect their desire to employ you. Some employers, depending on the industry, prefer not to hire employees who have criminal records.

Contact Us

Call us at (972) 943-8500.

For more information about our law firm, our team, and our experience trying DWI cases, visit us at DeandraGrantLaw.com or watch our videos at DeandraGrant.tv.

Our Cooke County office location:
1317 E McKinney St., Suite 101
Denton, TX 76029

Made in the USA
Monee, IL
04 November 2026

67384593R00015

SURVIVING YOUR DWI

in Tarrant County

Deandra M. Grant, JD, GC, MS
ACS-CHAL Forensic Lawyer-Scientist
Managing Partner

Douglas E. Huff, JD
ACS-CHAL Forensic Lawyer-Scientist
Partner

Offices Conveniently Located in
Dallas | Denton | Austin | Allen | Fort Worth | Waco

ISBNS:
PAPERBACK: 978-1-964281-07-0
EBOOK: 978-1-964281-06-3

DISCLAIMER

The information in this book does NOT constitute legal advice. You can only obtain sound legal advice from a lawyer who has been given the specific facts of your case. Every case is different.

Please note that our lawyers are happy to consult with you if you do decide to obtain legal advice. However, please understand that simply reading this book does not form an attorney-client relationship with our firm or with any of the authors.

Table of Contents

Meet the Authors

Meet Deandra M. Grant, JD, GC, MS:

Deandra M. Grant

Deandra Grant was born in Denton, but grew up in Plano, and is a proud graduate of Plano Senior High School. A native Texan, her family has lived for generations in and around Gainesville, Texas.

Deandra's hard-nosed work ethic began at an early age with a variety of teenage jobs: social director at a teen nightclub, clerk at a dress shop, and owner/manager of a New Orleans-style sno-cone stand (Mr Sno Ball!), to name a few.

After high school she attended Trinity University in San Antonio, then came back home to Dallas for law school at SMU. Deandra has been married to Eric Clendenin for over 20 years and they have two children, Keegan and Rowan.

When not practicing law, she is very involved with dog rescue and serves as vice president of Living the Doxie Dream Rescue & Sanctuary, in Royse City. At home she and Eric have five rescue dachshunds, and you can follow their adventures on their Instagram page, @5WienerPack.

Deandra is a huge Van Halen fan (DLR – not Hagar), studies medieval European history as a hobby, and loves to travel.

Lawyer Stuff:

Deandra was included in the list of Super Lawyers® for 2011, 2012, and 2015 through 2023. Super Lawyers is an attorney rating service that is nationally recognized throughout the legal community. After performing exhaustive and rigorous research by an independent research team, they announce their list of highly capable, trustworthy, and competent attorneys in *Super Lawyers* magazine and online. The list represents no more than 5% of the attorneys in Texas.

Deandra is AV Preeminent Rated by Martindale-Hubbell, which is the highest rating an attorney can achieve. She was given the AV rating for her outstanding professional achievements in the field of DWI law and her contributions to the legal community. She's also been rated 10.0 by both AVVO and Justia.

Deandra began work on *The Texas DWI Manual* in 2011 for James Publishing. She calls it her "labor of love." The first edition was released in 2013. It is updated annually and is considered a "must have" for attorneys defending DWI cases in Texas.

Experience

Deandra graduated in 1990 from Trinity University in San Antonio with a B.S. in Business Administration. She earned her law degree from the SMU School of Law and was licensed by the State Bar of Texas in 1993. Having spent her last year of law school as an intern with the Dallas County District Attorney's Office, she began work there as an assistant district attorney in January 1994.

Deandra's tenure as a prosecutor focused on DWI prosecution. In 1995, she founded her own firm and began defending citizens accused of DWI and other crimes. She has practiced criminal defense for over 30 years and represents Texans charged with criminal offenses, including DWI, violent felonies, and sex crimes. As a former prosecutor, she knows firsthand how to counter the prosecutor's evidence and strategy.

Operator and Testing Experience

Deandra has spent hundreds of hours in training courses and programs related to DWI defense. She has participated in numerous "dosing" experiments in which people are given specific amounts of alcohol over certain time periods and then tested to see the effect of the alcohol on their mental and physical capabilities. She attended and successfully completed the operator certification course for the Intoxilyzer 5000 in Florida in 2004. This was the breath-test machine used in Texas prior to the purchase of the Intoxilyzer 9000. She learned how to operate the machine and the science behind it. She has also participated in experiments related to the inaccuracy of the machine.

Deandra has completed both the student course (2008) and the instructor course (2009) on the administration of standardized field sobriety testing (SFST), the same National Highway Traffic Safety Administration training course that teaches police officers nationwide how to identify drunk drivers during traffic stops. She now serves as an instructor of the SFST practitioner course to share the knowledge with other attorneys. In 2008, she completed coursework in Atlanta, Georgia, on DWI forensic blood and urine testing.

In 2011, she began training at Axion Labs in Chicago. The courses include Forensic Chromatography, Forensic Drug Analysis, and Forensic Driving Under the Influence of Drugs. She completed the coursework, passed the final exam in

2015, and was awarded the American Chemical Society Forensic Lawyer-Scientist designation. In 2018, Deandra joined Axion Labs as an assistant chromatography instructor. She spends five weeks each year in Chicago at the lab.

In 2014, Deandra "went back to school." She completed a Graduate Certificate in Forensic Toxicology from the University of Florida's College of Veterinary Medicine, and a master's degree in Pharmaceutical Science – Concentration in Forensic Science from the University of Florida's College of Pharmacy, in 2016.

Deandra is a national speaker and teacher on topics including trial skills, jury selection, cross examination, field sobriety tests, drugged driving, and forensic breath and blood alcohol testing. Since 2019, she's been honored to serve on the faculty of the Robert F. Borkenstein Course on the Effects of Drugs on Human Performance and Behavior.

Meet Douglas E. Huff, JD:

Douglas E. Huff

Attorney Douglas Huff was born in Warren, Ohio, and was raised in Western Pennsylvania, outside of Pittsburgh, where he attended Mount Pleasant Area High School. After high school, Attorney Huff enlisted in the United States Army and served for four years, receiving both the Army Achievement Medal and the Army Commendation Medal. He received an honorable discharge after completing his full term of service and relocated to Austin, Texas.

After attending law school, Doug worked at Barbri, an organization specializing in assisting law students in studying and passing the state bar examination. In addition to being licensed to practice law in the state of Texas, he sat and passed the Oklahoma Bar during this time. Afterward, he opened his own law practice, The Law Office of Douglas E. Huff, in Dallas, Texas, where he represented clients charged with various misdemeanor and felony criminal offenses.

In 2013, Doug accepted a position with the Dallas County Public Defender's Office, where he worked diligently as the lead attorney in many DWI trials and other misdemeanor cases. Additionally, he has assisted numerous clients through plea negotiations, led many evidentiary hearings, and prepared and taken part in felony trials.

Attorney Huff joined Deandra Grant Law in 2016. He became a partner in 2021. Doug is based in the Dallas office, but practices throughout Texas.

On a personal note, Doug has one daughter (attorney Sorsha Huff) and a rescue dog named Athena. He's a military vet who loves to travel. One of his favorite trips was walking the Camino de Santiago, in Spain. Doug is also a competitive poker player whom you can often find playing in tournaments around the country.

Introduction

So, you've been arrested for DWI in Tarrant County and you're wondering, "What next?"

This book walks you through the steps you need to take to deal with both the driver's license issues and criminal charges you face.

County Information

Tim Curry Justice Center
401 W Belknap St
Fort Worth, TX 76196
Bond Supervision (817) 884-1600

MISDEMEANOR COURTS:

County Criminal Court #1	(817) 884-1337	5th floor
County Criminal Court #2	(817) 884-1338	6th floor
County Criminal Court #3	(817) 884-1374	7th floor
County Criminal Court #4	(817) 884-1426	5th floor
County Criminal Court #5	(817) 884-2726	6th floor
County Criminal Court #6	(817) 884-2745	8th floor
County Criminal Court #7	(817) 884-2773	8th floor
County Criminal Court #8	(817) 884-3400	7th floor
County Criminal Court #9	(817) 884-3410	8th floor
County Criminal Court #10	(817) 884-3420	6th floor

FELONY COURTS:

Criminal District Court #1	(817) 884-1351	5th floor
Criminal District Court #2	(817) 884-1347	6th floor
Criminal District Court #3	(817) 884-1356	7th floor
Criminal District Court #4	(817) 884-1362	8th floor
213th Criminal District Court	(817) 884-1529	5th floor
297th Criminal District Court	(817) 884-1908	5th floor
371st Criminal District Court	(817) 884-2985	5th floor
372nd Criminal District Court	(817) 884-2990	6th floor
396th Criminal District Court	(817) 884-2768	6th floor
432nd Criminal District Court	(817) 884-2335	6th floor

What to Expect

Step #1: Department of Public Safety

- Make sure the address on your driver's license is correct. If it's not, you need to go to the DPS website and update your address.

- Check your mail regularly for letters from the Department of Public Safety (DPS).

The DPS will mail any letters to you at the address they have on file. If you have moved, or don't frequently check your mail, you could miss time-sensitive letters regarding your right to challenge the suspension of your driver's license, which can aggravate your situation.

We often see new clients who, prior to coming to us, have already missed their opportunity to challenge a driver's license suspension following a DWI arrest, either because the DPS did not have their correct address when mailing a notice of the hearing or the client did not regularly check incoming mail. Too often, these clients are unaware that they are driving with a suspended license until they are caught and charged.

Step #2: Tarrant County Bond Conditions

- Comply with any and all bond conditions ordered by the judge who sets your bond.

If there was an accident, a breath or blood alcohol content result of 0.15 or greater, or if you have had prior DWIs, the judge will likely order that a deep lung device (DLD) be installed on any car that you drive. You MUST contact the Bond Supervision Department within the timeframe noted on your court order/bond conditions and set up an appointment. You are required to pay to have the unit installed and provide proof to your bond supervision officer. You will also be required to report in, and pay a monthly supervision fee, while your case is pending.

We sometimes have clients who were involved in accidents and no longer have a car to drive. In that case, your bond supervision officer will likely order that an alcohol monitoring device be installed in your home instead of your car. You will be required to blow into this device at specific times in order to demonstrate that you are not drinking alcohol while on bond.

Failure to comply with bond conditions can lead to your bond being held insufficient and a warrant issued for your arrest.

If you took a breath test and the result was 0.15 or greater, OR if you had blood drawn and the result was 0.15 or greater, but an interlock device was NOT added as a condition of bond when you bonded out of jail, do not be surprised if, at your first court appearance, the judge handling your criminal case orders you to install one.

Step #3: Administrative License Revocation

- Request an ALR hearing within 15 days

If you refused to provide a specimen of your breath or blood after your DWI arrest, you have 15 days from the date you received notice of suspension to request a hearing. Notice of suspension is typically handed to you by the police officer or included in your paperwork when you bond out of jail.

If you consented to a blood test, the clock doesn't start ticking until the Department of Public Safety (DPS) sends you a notice of suspension. However, we see a lot of mistakes made by officers, such as labeling your charge a "failure," meaning you refused to consent to a test when in fact your blood was taken with your consent. That mistake can cost you.

You can request the hearing yourself, or your attorney can request it for you. If you fail to request the hearing within the 15-day timeframe, however, your right to a hearing is forfeit and your license will be suspended on the 40th day after notice of suspension was served.

Step #4: Tarrant County Court Appearances

- Establish when and where you are required to appear in court

Tarrant County has 10 county (misdemeanor case) and 10 district (felony case) courts, all located in the Tim Curry Justice Center. See the preceding chapter for a directory indicating which courts are on which floors.

Tarrant County judges typically require you to appear at all court settings, even if charged in misdemeanor court.

It is not uncommon in Tarrant for there to be a large number of cases on each docket, so plan to be in court for most of the morning. Cases in Tarrant County tend to move faster than those in surrounding counties.

Step #5: Disposition Meeting

- Meet with your attorney to decide how to proceed

At Deandra Grant Law, we first write a case evaluation that summarizes all of the evidence in the case for you and gives you our overall opinion of your case. Once you have had the opportunity to review our case evaluation and watch any videos from your arrest, we schedule a disposition meeting where we sit down with you to discuss achieving the best outcome for you. At that meeting, we decide together whether that best outcome is to accept a plea bargain or take your case to trial.

Step #6: Plea Docket or Trial Docket

- Schedule a plea date or a trial date, depending on how you decide to proceed with your case, and appear on the scheduled date and time

After your disposition meeting, it is time to schedule either a plea date or a trial date. You must appear on all plea or trial dates.

Plea Date

If you choose to enter into a plea bargain with the State, you must appear at the Tim Curry Justice Center on your plea court date.

Take a seat in the courtroom and wait for your attorney to arrive. Once the plea paperwork is completed, you enter your plea in front of the judge. It might be the presiding judge or a visiting judge who takes your plea.

If you are placed on probation, you will meet with a probation officer after you enter your plea and the clerks complete your paperwork. The clerks and probation officer are normally in the courtroom during the plea.

The whole process takes several hours, so plan to be at the courthouse until noon or later.

Trial Announcement

Cases on the trial docket will be set for a trial announcement date, which is normally scheduled one to two weeks before the trial date. At trial announcement, both the State (prosecution) and the Defense will announce "Ready" or "Not Ready" for trial. The judge will also likely handle any pre-trial issues/rulings that need to be made before the trial begins.

At trial announcement, the judge will let the attorneys know which cases are likely to go to trial during the scheduled trial week and which ones will be rescheduled.

Trial Date

On your trial date you must appear no later than 9 a.m. (or earlier if ordered by the judge) and wait for your attorney to meet you in court.

If your case is reached, your trial will normally begin that day and may last one to three days, depending on many factors.

DWI FAQs

Q: **When I was arrested for DWI in Tarrant County, I received a piece of paper that said my driver's license is suspended. Is my license now suspended?**

A: No. *You have 15 days from the date you are served your Notice of Suspension to request an administrative license revocation (ALR) hearing regarding your driver's license.* If you do not request a hearing, your license will be suspended on the 40th day after Notice of Suspension is served. It is important to seek the advice of an attorney regarding your driver's license issues before this 15-day window expires.

If you consented to a blood draw, a Notice of Suspension will be mailed to you if the DPS (Department of Public Safety) receives notice that your blood alcohol analysis resulted in an alcohol concentration of 0.08 or greater. *Once you receive this Notice of Suspension letter from DPS, you only have 20 days from the date of the letter to request an ALR hearing.* If you do not request a hearing, your license will be suspended on the 45th day from the date on the Notice of Suspension letter.

Q: For my DWI arrest, I was ordered to install a deep lung device (DLD) on my car as a condition of bond. What do I have to do, and is that my only option?

A: In certain circumstances, a DLD may be required while your case is pending. There may be alternatives that would work for you. We can tell you more when we sit down with you to examine the specific circumstances of your case.

Q: When do I have to go to court on my DWI for the first time, if it's a misdemeanor case?

A: In Tarrant County, misdemeanor cases are normally filed rather quickly, so you can expect to have a court date fairly soon after you post bond. You will need to retain an attorney before your first court appearance.

Q: How long will it take to resolve my DWI case in Tarrant County?

A: There are many factors that determine how long a criminal case will last. Cases that are on the trial docket obviously take longer to resolve than cases where a plea bargain is worked out. The majority of our DWI cases are resolved within six to 12 months in Tarrant County.

Q: Will I go to prison or jail for my DWI?

A: The punishment varies, depending upon the circumstances of your particular case, and whether this is your first, second, or subsequent offense. When you work with a defense lawyer and fight your charges, you may have the opportunity to avoid a conviction and remain free.

Q: How can an attorney help me with my DWI in Tarrant County?

A: An attorney works knowledgeably and skillfully to protect your rights and interests by challenging the prosecution's case and the evidence against you. This may include challenges to field sobriety test results, breath test results, or blood test results. An attorney's representation also includes being present, either at your side or on your behalf, at any and all court appearances, including trial.

An attorney will also work on your driver's license issues and help you deal with any possible license suspension.

Q: Can a lawyer represent me at my Tarrant County ALR hearing?

A: Yes. We can contact the Department of Public Safety to schedule your administrative license revocation (ALR) hearing and represent you at the hearing in order to help you reach a better outcome. Your driving privileges are extremely important, and skilled representation at your hearing may mean the difference between you keeping those privileges or losing them.

Q: What are some penalties associated with a Tarrant County DWI conviction?

A: Specific penalties vary, but, in general, a defendant may face imprisonment, probation, community service, driver's license suspension, fines, and more.

Q: If I have a DWI conviction on my record, can this affect my ability to find employment?

A: It is possible that having a DWI conviction on your criminal record may make it more difficult for you to find employment. When a potential employer conducts a pre-employment background search, your DWI conviction will show up. This may or may not affect their desire to employ you. Some employers, depending on the industry, prefer not to hire employees who have criminal records.

Contact Us

Call us at (972) 943-8500.

For more information about our law firm, our team, and our experience trying DWI cases, visit us at DeandraGrantLaw.com or watch our videos at DeandraGrant.tv.

Our Tarrant County office location:
4500 Airport Freeway, Suite 101
Fort Worth, TX 76117

Made in the USA
Monee, IL
04 November 2026

67384571R00015